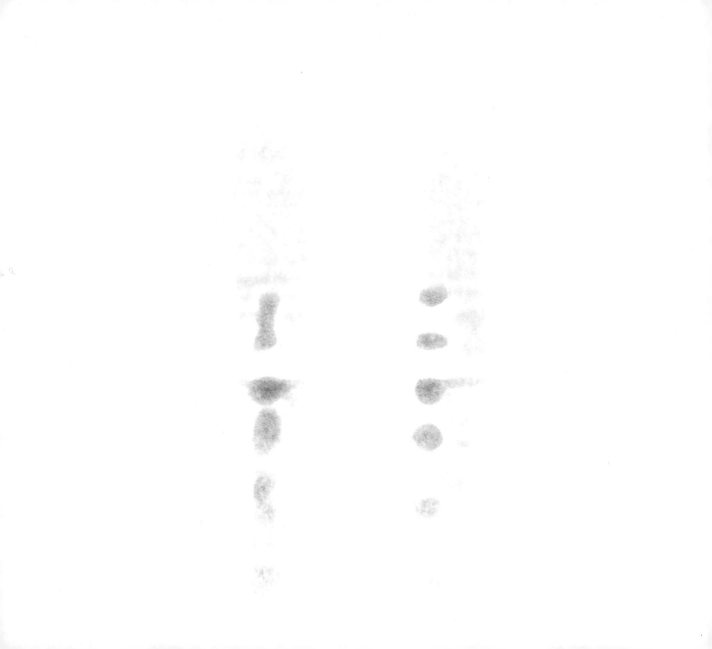

HOLIDAYS AND FESTIVALS

Independence Day

Rebecca Rissman

Heinemann Library
Chicago, Illinois

www.heinemannraintree.com
Visit our website to find out
more information about
Heinemann-Raintree books.

To order:

☎ Phone 888-454-2279

💻 Visit www.heinemannraintree.com
to browse our catalog and order online.

©2011 Heinemann Library
an imprint of Capstone Global Library, LLC
Chicago, Illinois

Edited by Adrian Vigliano and Rebecca Rissman
Designed by Ryan Frieson
Picture research by Tracy Cummins
Leveling by Nancy E. Harris
Originated by Capstone Global Library Ltd.
Printed in China by South China Printing Company Ltd.

15 14 13 12 11 10
10 9 8 7 6 5 4 3 2 1

Library of Congress Cataloging-in-Publication Data
Rissman, Rebecca.
  Independence Day / Rebecca Rissman.
    p. cm.—(Holidays and festivals)
  Includes bibliographical references and index.
  ISBN 978-1-4329-4060-7 (hc)—ISBN 978-1-4329-4079-9 (pbk.) 1. Fourth
of July—Juvenile literature. 2. Fourth of July celebrations—Juvenile
literature. I. Title.
  E286.A162 2010
  394.263—dc22   2009052864

Acknowledgments

The author and publishers are grateful to the following for permission
to reproduce copyright material: Corbis ©Ariel Skelley **p.4**; Corbis
©Steve Cicero **p.5**; Corbis ©Bettmann **p.13**; Corbis ©Bob Daemmrich
p.21; Getty Images/Jeff Corwin **p.19**; istockphoto ©Sean Locke **p.16**;
istockphoto ©Leo Blanchette **p.22**; Library of Congress Prints and
Photographs Division **p.14**; Shutterstock ©Suzanne Tucker **p.17**;
Shutterstock ©Moritz Frei **p.18**; Shutterstock © Karla Caspari **p.20**;
The Bridgeman Art Library International ©Look and Learn **p.6**; The
Bridgeman Art Library International ©The Berwick Collection, Shropshire,
UK/National Trust Photographic Library/John Hammond **p.8, 23c**;
The Bridgeman Art Library International ©Collection of the New-York
Historical Society, USA **p.10**; The Bridgeman Art Library International
©Peter Newark American Pictures **pp.12, 23b**; The Granger Collection,
New York **pp.9**, **11**, **15**, **23a**, **23d**.

Cover photograph of July 4th Fireworks, New York reproduced with
permission of Getty Images/Jumper. Back cover photograph reproduced
with permission of Shutterstock ©Suzanne Tucker.

Every effort has been made to contact copyright holders of any material
reproduced in this book. Any omissions will be rectified in subsequent
printings if notice is given to the publisher.

Contents

What Is a Holiday?

A holiday is a special day.
People celebrate holidays.

Independence Day is a holiday.
Independence Day is in July.

The Story of Independence Day

In the 1600s, people from England sailed to America. They settled there.

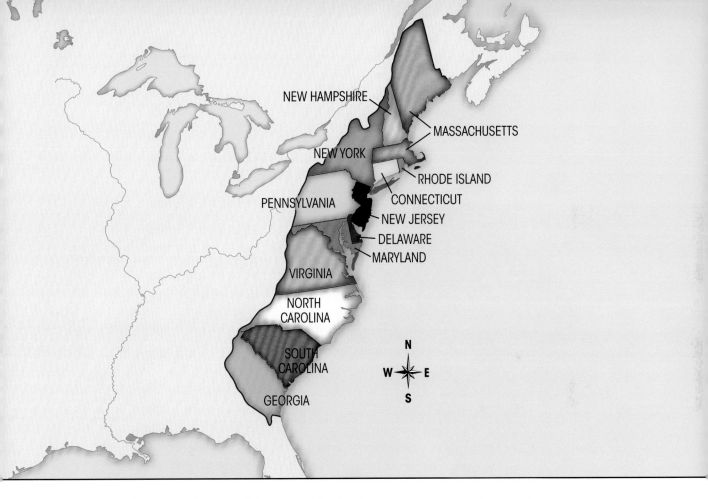

They lived in the thirteen colonies. The colonies were groups of people that were ruled by the King of England.

The King made the colonies pay taxes to England.

The people in the colonies felt this was not fair.

9

The people in the colonies wanted to become free. They wanted to become a new country.

The King of England did not want the colonies to become free. England and the colonies went to war in 1775.

The colonists wrote the Declaration of Independence. It said that the colonies would be a new country.

The Declaration of Independence was finished on July 4, 1776. This was the first Independence Day.

The colonists won the Revolutionary War in 1781.

The colonies became the United States of America in 1783. And the colonists became Americans.

Celebrating Independence Day

On Independence Day people celebrate America.

16

People watch parades.

People watch fireworks.

People give thanks for their freedom.

Independence Day Symbols

People fly the American flag on Independence Day.

The American flag is a symbol
of freedom.

Calendar

Independence Day is on July 4.

Picture Glossary

 **colonies** groups of people that are ruled by another country

 **independence** to be free

 **king** the ruler in some countries

 **war** a fight between two or more countries or groups

Index

Note to Parents and Teachers

Before reading
Explain that every year on July 4, Americans celebrate Independence Day. Ask the children to share their Independence Day experiences. Briefly explain that this holiday isn't just a time for picnics and fireworks, but also a time when Americans celebrate the "birthday" of their country. Sing a rousing chorus of "Happy Birthday."

After reading
Create an Independence Day parade. Gather craft materials and have the children make streamers, hats, banners, flags, and other parade-like accessories. Bring portable music and strike up the band. Take your parade on the road by marching around the classroom, the house, or the playground.

24